# TEXAS

## SCIENCE FUSION

## Write-In Student Edition

Houghton Mifflin Harcourt

**Front Cover:** *penguins* ©Paul Souders/Corbis; *top* ©Image Source/Alamy; *ladybug* ©Radius Images/Alamy; *earth* ©Chris Walsh/Getty Images; *magnet* ©mauritius images GmbH/Alamy; *paper clips* ©moodboard/Alamy

**Back Cover:** *tulips* ©John McAnulty/Corbis; *soccer* ©Jon Feingersh Photography Inc/Blend Images/Getty Images; *volcano* ©Westend 6I GmbH/Alamy; *microscope* ©Thom Lang/Corbis.

Printed in the U.S.A.

ISBN 978-0-544-02545-5

8 9 10 11 12 0877 21 20 19 18 17

4500647838        BCDEFG

# Contents

# Safety in Science

## Indoors

Be safe indoors.
Follow these rules.

**safe eyes**

1 **Think ahead.** Follow these steps.

2 **Be neat.** Wipe up spills right away. Keep hair and clothing out of the way.

3 **Oops!** Tell your teacher if you spill or break something. Tell your teacher if you get hurt.

4 **Watch your eyes.** Wear safety goggles when the teacher tells you.

5 **Ouch!** Do not touch sharp things.

6 **Yuck!** Do not eat or drink things.

7 **Do not touch electric outlets.**

8 **Keep it clean.** Clean up afterward. Wash your hands with soap and water to stay healthy.

**TEKS** **K.1A** identify and demonstrate safe practices as described in the Texas Safety Standards during classroom and outdoor investigations, including wearing safety goggles, washing hands, and using materials appropriately **K.1B** discuss the importance of safe practices to keep self and others safe and healthy

# Safety in Science

## Outdoors
Be safe outdoors.
Follow these rules.

**safe clothes and shoes**

1. **Think ahead.** Follow these steps.

2. **Dress right.** Wear clothes and shoes that are right for outdoors.

3. **Oops!** Tell your teacher if you break something or get hurt.

4. **Watch your eyes.** Tell your teacher if anything gets in your eyes.

5. **Yuck!** Never taste things outdoors.

6. **Stay together on marked trails.**

7. **Do not act wild.** No horseplay.

8. **Clean up the area.** Throw away litter as your teacher tells you.

9. **Clean up.** Afterward, wash your hands with soap and water to stay healthy.

© Houghton Mifflin Harcourt Publishing Company.

# Our Senses

touch

smell

hear

see

taste

TEKS **K.2D** record and organize data and observations using pictures, numbers, and words **K.4B** use senses as a tool of observation to identify properties and patterns of organisms, objects, and events in the environment

Unit 1 • Lesson 1
How Do We Use Our Senses?

1

Name _____

**see**

**hear**

Draw.

Your senses help you learn.
You see things with your eyes.
You hear sounds with your ears.

▶ Draw something you see (observe). What can you tell about the way the object looks?

Name _____

**touch**

**smell**

**taste**

You touch things with your hands and skin.
You smell things with your nose.
You taste foods with your mouth.

▶ Circle the body part the girl is using to smell the flower.

# Sum It Up!

● Circle the child hearing something.  ▲ Circle the child seeing something.  ■ Circle the child tasting something.

# Science Skills

**observe**

**compare**

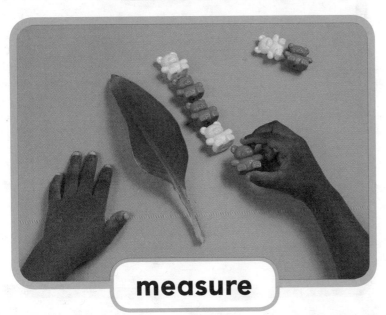

**measure**

big     small

**sort**

**TEKS** **K.2A** ask questions about organisms, objects, and events observed in the natural world **K.2D** record and organize data and observations using pictures, numbers, and words **K.4A** collect information using non-standard measuring items such as paper clips . . .

**measure**

Draw.

**observe**

We ask questions to learn.
We observe to find answers.
We measure to find answers.

▶ Use your eyes to observe your hand. What can you tell about how your hand looks? Draw what you observe. Compare pictures with classmates. Then tell how many paper clips long the paintbrush is.

Name _____

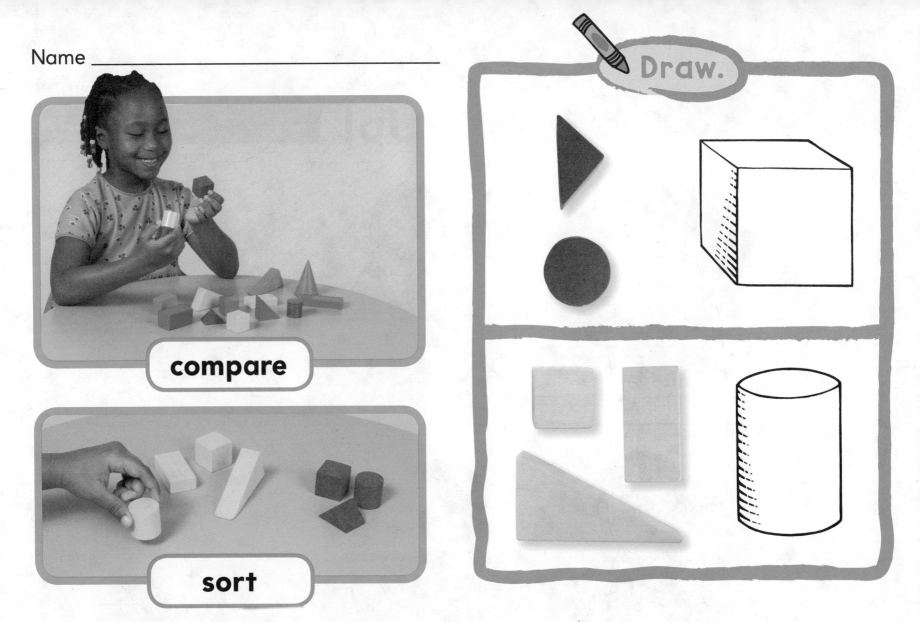

**compare**

**sort**

We compare how things are alike and different.
We sort things that are alike into groups.

▶ Color each block to match its group.

# Sum It Up!

● Circle the child measuring something.
▲ Circle the child sorting things.

# Science Tools

hand lens

thermometer

balance

measuring cup

ruler

**TEKS** **K.2C** collect data and make observations using simple equipment such as hand lenses, primary balances, and non-standard measurement tools **K.2D** record and organize data and observations using pictures, numbers, and words **K.3C** explore that scientists investigate different things in the natural world and use tools to help in their investigations **K.4A** collect information using tools, including ... hand lenses, primary balances, cups ... ; weather instruments such as demonstration thermometers ...

Name _____

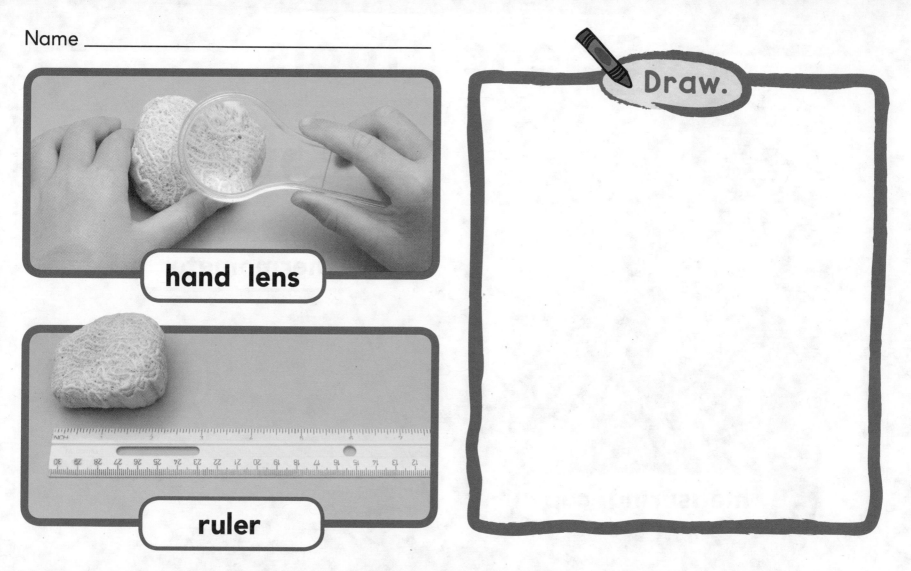

**hand lens**

**ruler**

Draw.

We use science tools to learn about things.
A hand lens makes things look bigger.
A ruler shows how long something is.

▶ Draw an object. Then draw what that object would look like through a hand lens. Draw a line under the ruler. Tell what you can measure with a ruler.

Name _____

**balance**

**thermometer**

**measuring cup**

A balance shows which thing is heavier.

A thermometer shows how warm it is.

A measuring cup shows how much water.

# Sum It Up!

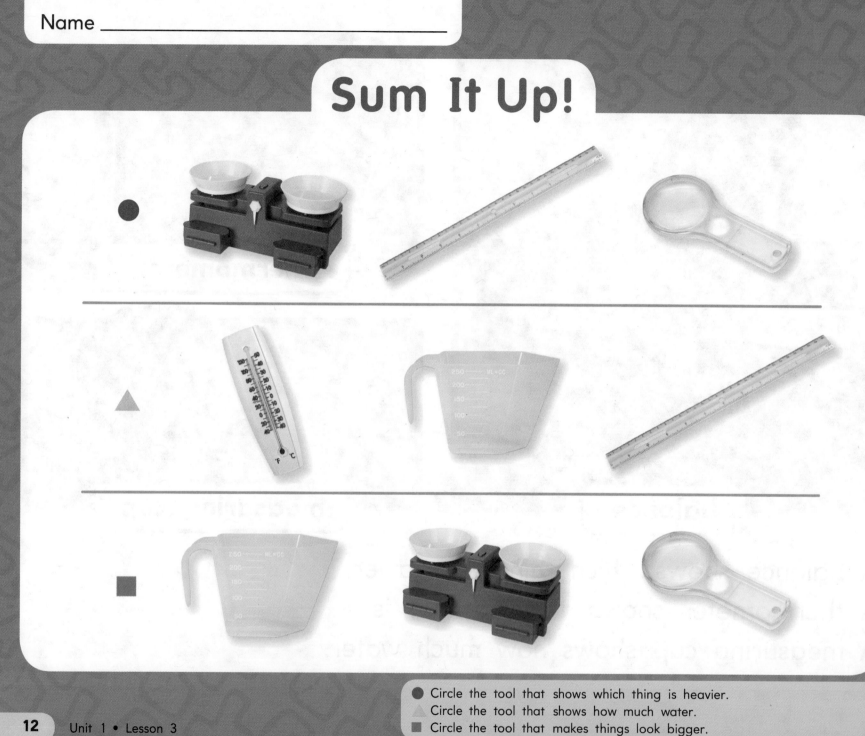

● Circle the tool that shows which thing is heavier.
▲ Circle the tool that shows how much water.
■ Circle the tool that makes things look bigger.

# Solving Problems

engineer

**TEKS** **K.2D** record and organize data and observations using pictures, numbers, and words **K.3A** identify and explain a problem … and propose a solution in his/her own words.

Name _____

Engineers solve problems.

They design buildings and roads.

They design things we use at home.

▶ Draw a circle around the engineers.

Name _____

**Draw.**

You can design things too.

▶ Identify and explain what the child's problem might be. Discuss what he can do. Draw what the boy might design and build with the blocks.

# Sum It Up!

▶ Draw lines to match each problem to how an engineer solved the problem.

# Design Process

**problem**

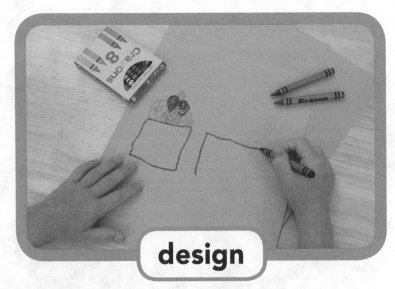

**design**

**solve**

**TEKS** **K.1C** demonstrate how to use, conserve, and dispose of natural resources and materials such as conserving water and reusing or recycling paper, plastic, and metal **K.2D** record and organize data and observations using pictures, numbers, and words **K.3A** identify and explain a problem … and propose a solution in his/her own words

**Find a problem.**

A design process is a plan with steps.
The steps can help you solve a problem.
The first step is to find the problem.

▶ Identify and explain the problem. Circle the problem.

Name _____

**Plan and build.**

Think of a way to solve the problem.
Design a plan. Then build it.

▶ Identify the girl's solution to the problem. Circle it.

**Test.**

**Improve.**

Test your plan.

Does your plan solve the problem?

Can you make your plan better?

▶ Tell how the girl improved her plan.

**Redesign. Talk about it.**

Draw.

Change your plan to make it better.
Talk with others about it.

▶ Propose another solution to the girl's problem. Draw a picture of it.
Explain your solution in your own words.

# Sum It Up!

▶ The steps are not in order. Draw a line under the first step of the design process. Circle the last step of the design process.

# Matter

matter

**TEKS** **K.2D** record and organize data and observations using pictures, numbers, and words **K.5A** observe and record properties of objects, including relative size and mass, such as bigger or smaller and heavier or lighter, shape, color, and texture

**liquid**

**gas**

**solid**

Matter is anything that takes up space.
Matter can be a liquid, a gas, or a solid.

▶ Draw an X on the liquid.

Name _____

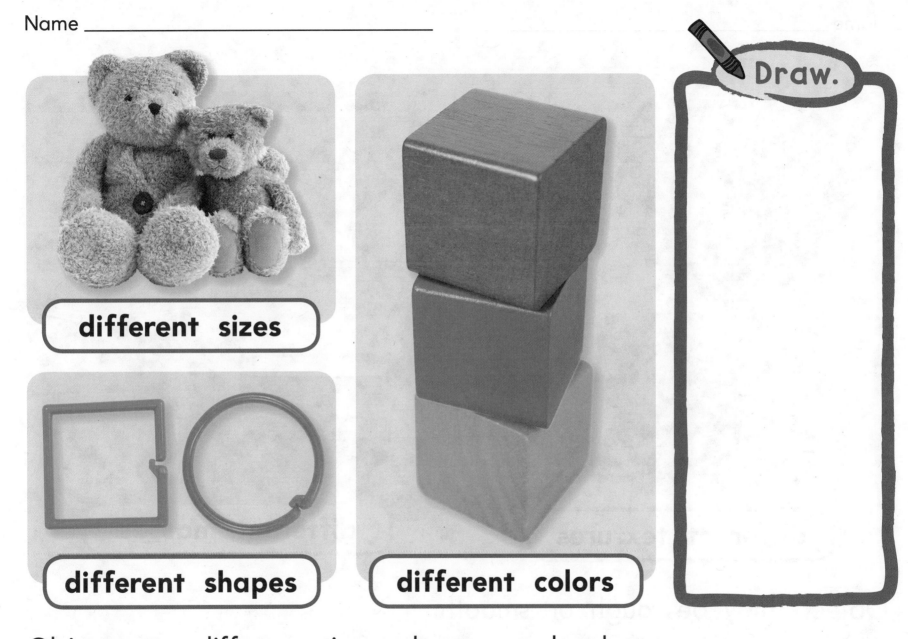

**different sizes**

**different shapes**

**different colors**

Draw.

Objects are different sizes, shapes, and colors.

► Observe the bears. Circle the bigger bear. Draw two blocks. Make one block bigger than the other. Circle the smaller block.

Name _____

**different textures**

**different masses**

Objects may be rough or smooth.
Objects may be heavy or light.

▶ Circle the rough shell. Underline the smooth shell.
Draw an X on the book that has more mass.

Name _____

**different temperatures**

Things may be hot or cold.

▶ Draw a cold drink you like.

Draw.

# Sum It Up!

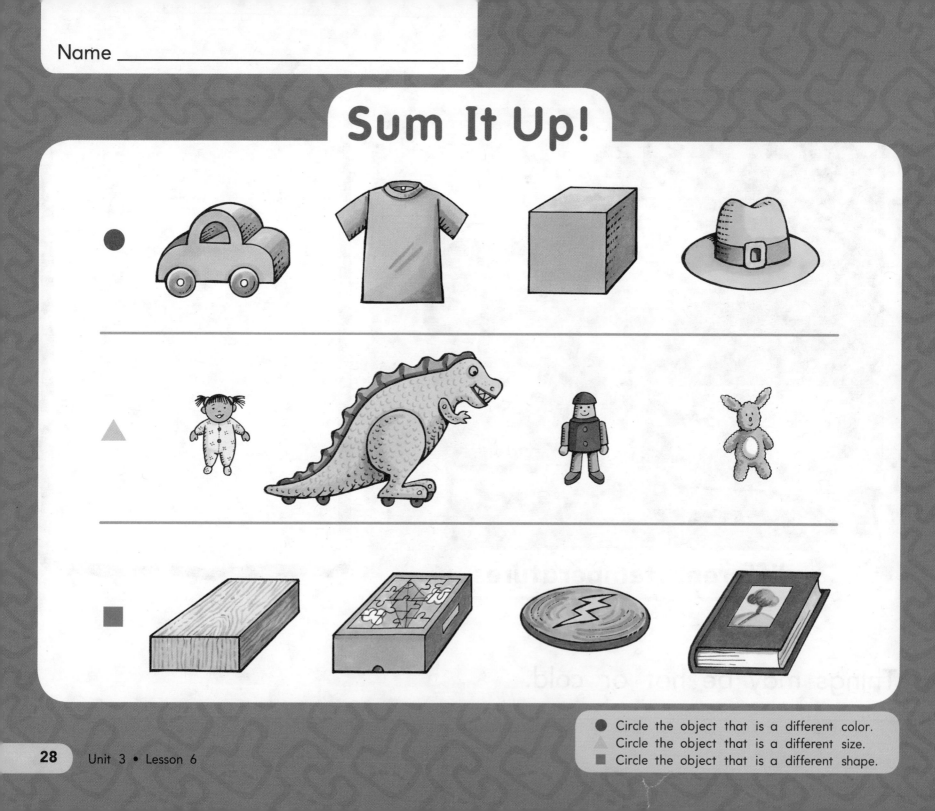

● Circle the object that is a different color.
▲ Circle the object that is a different size.
■ Circle the object that is a different shape.

# Heating and Cooling Matter

heat

cool

**TEKS** **K.4B** use senses as a tool of observation to identify properties and patterns of organisms, objects, and events in the environment **K.5B** observe, record, and discuss how materials can be changed by heating or cooling

Name _____

**heating**

Draw.

**raw egg**

**cooked egg**

Matter may change when it heats up.

© Houghton Mifflin Harcourt Publishing Company    (l) ©Bloom Works Inc./Alamy; (r) ©Beyond Fotomedia GmbH/Alamy

▶ Observe how the egg is changed by heating. Draw (record) how the egg looks after it is cooked. Discuss how eggs and other materials can be changed by heating.

Name _____

**liquid**

**cooling**

**solid**

When matter cools, it may change.
A liquid may become a solid.

▶ Observe how the liquid is being changed by cooling. Circle (record) the
matter being cooled. Discuss how water and other materials can be
changed by cooling.

# Sum It Up!

© Houghton Mifflin Harcourt Publishing Company

● Circle (record) what happens when water is cooled.
▲ Circle (record) what happens when pancake batter is heated.

# Light

light

**TEKS** **K.2D** record and organize data and observations using pictures, numbers, and words **K.6A** use the five senses to explore different forms of energy such as light, heat, and sound

Name _____

sun

lamp

**Draw.**

flashlight

The sun gives off light.
Some things people make give off light.
What other things give off light?

▶ Explore the sense you use to observe light. What gives off light in the classroom? What sense do you use to observe light? Draw something that gives off light.

Name _____

**very little light**

**a lot of light**

We need light to see things.

▶ Circle the room with more light. Discuss what happens when you close your eyes. Can you still observe light?

Name _____

# Sum It Up!

Circle the things that give off light. Tell what sense you use to observe light.

# Heat

heat

© Houghton Mifflin Harcourt Publishing Company  ©Photodisc/Getty Images

**TEKS** **K.2D** record and organize data and observations using pictures, numbers, and words **K.6A** use the five senses to explore different forms of energy, such as light, heat, and sound

Name _____

clothes dryer

toaster

Some things give off heat.

▶ Circle the thing that uses heat to toast bread. Discuss (explore) which sense you use to observe heat energy.

Name _____

**sun**

**candle**

**Draw.**

Many things give off both heat and light.

▶ Draw something that gives off heat and light. Tell the senses you use to observe heat and light.

# Sum It Up!

● ▲ ■ Circle the thing that gives off the <u>most</u> heat.

# Magnets

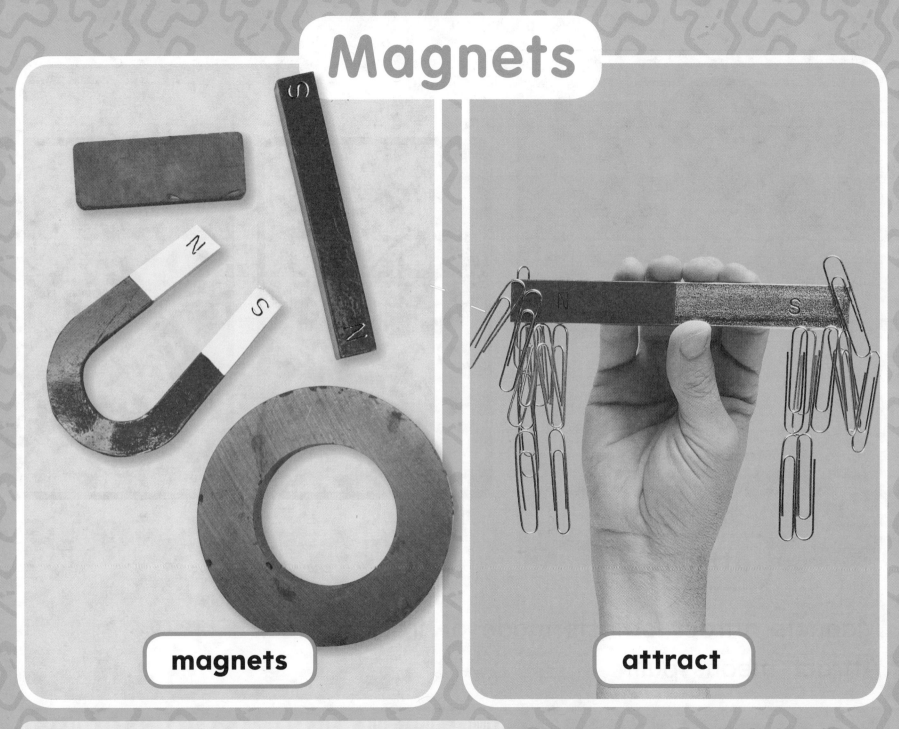

**magnets**

**attract**

© Houghton Mifflin Harcourt Publishing Company   (l) ©Leslie Garland Picture Library/Alamy

**TEKS** **K.2B** record and organize data and observations using pictures, numbers, and words **K.4A** collect information using tools, including . . . magnets . . . **K.6B** explore interactions between magnets and various materials

Unit 5 • Lesson 11
Which Objects Do Magnets Attract?   **47**

Name _____

**attract**

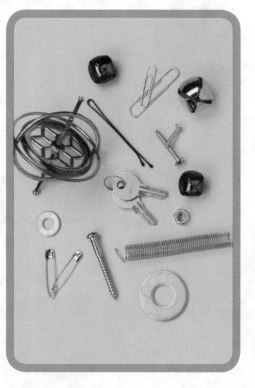

Magnets attract objects made of iron or steel.

Attract means pull.

▶ Explore what happens (explore interactions) between magnets and various materials. Circle the group of objects a magnet will attract.

Name _____

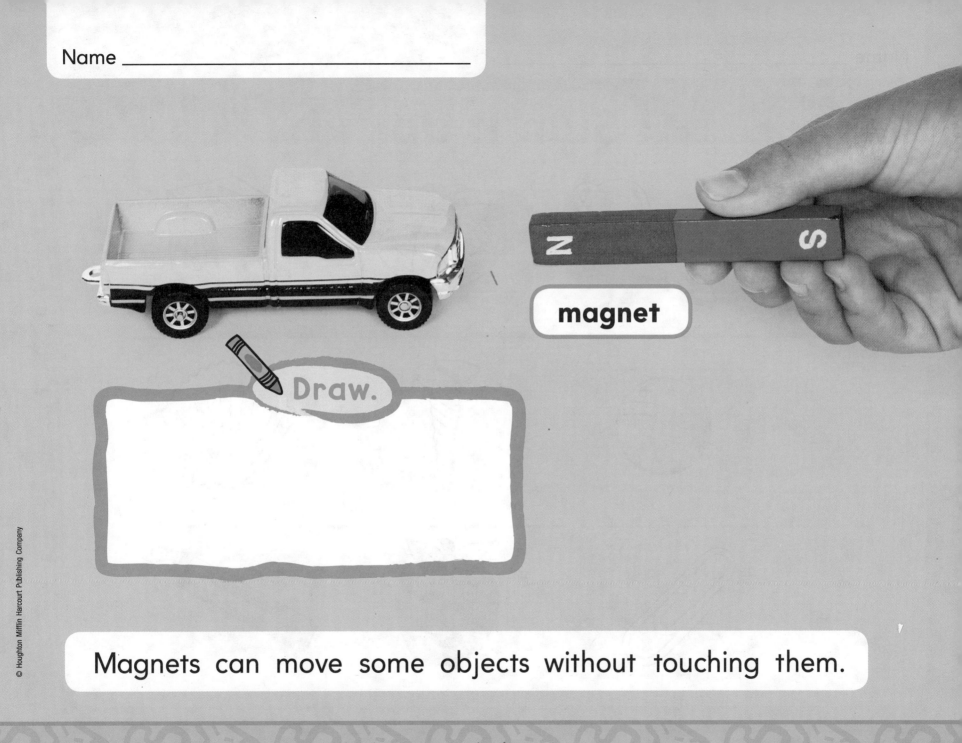

**magnet**

Draw.

Magnets can move some objects without touching them.

► Explore what happens when a magnet is placed near a toy made of iron or steel. Draw an arrow to show the direction the truck is moving.

Unit 5 • Lesson 11    49

Name _____

# Sum It Up!

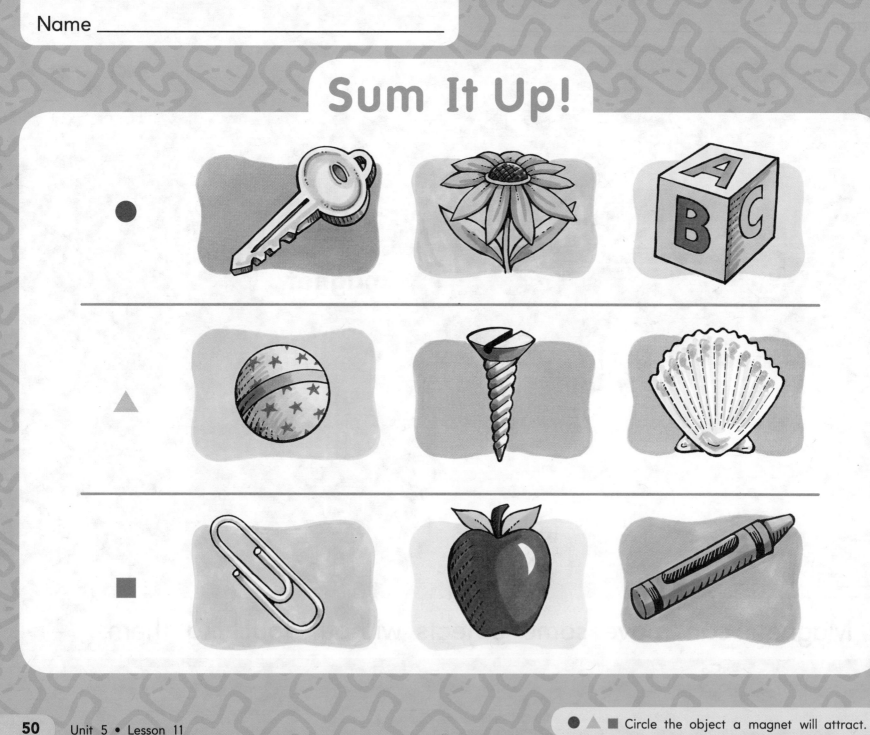

● ▲ ■ Circle the object a magnet will attract.

# Where Things Are

beside

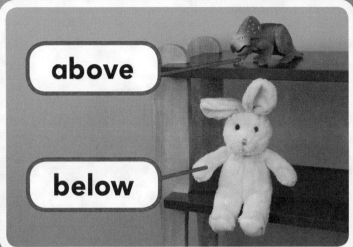

above

below

behind

in front of

© Houghton Mifflin Harcourt Publishing Company

Name _____

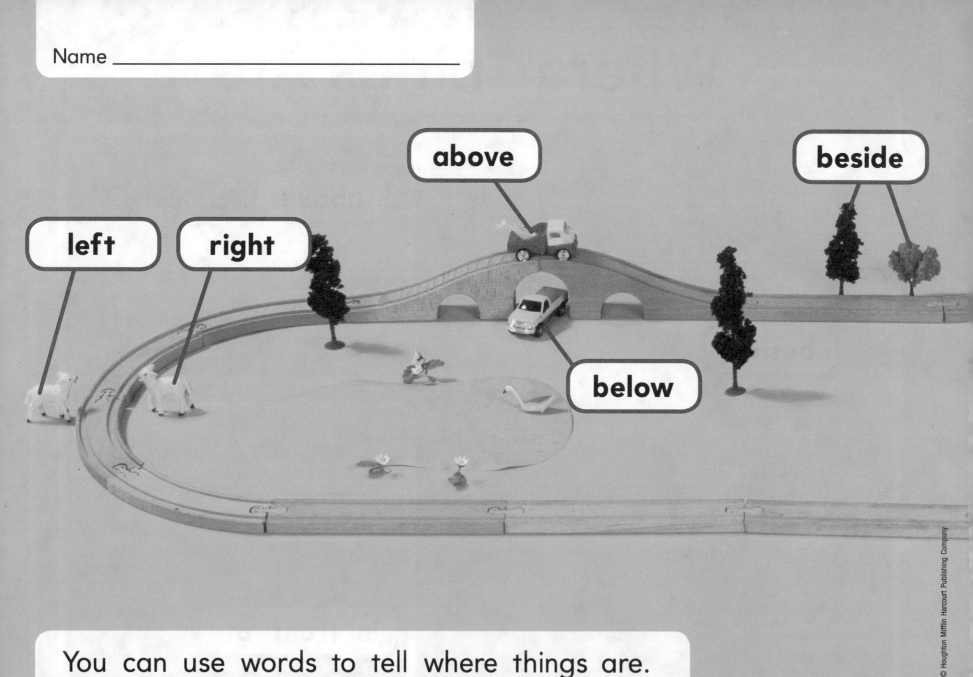

You can use words to tell where things are.

▶ Observe the locations of the objects on the two pages. Describe where the objects are in relation to one another. Circle the truck below the bridge.

Name _____

in

out

in front of

behind

Where are the ducks?

▶ Draw a ball with a tree behind it.

Name _____

# Sum It Up!

Color the toy above the airplane yellow. Color the toy below the truck blue. Color the toy beside the ball green. Color the toy in front of the basket orange.

© Houghton Mifflin Harcourt Publishing Company

# How Things Move

zigzag

up and down

round and round

straight

back and forth

© Houghton Mifflin Harcourt Publishing Company

**TEKS** **K.2B** plan and conduct simple descriptive investigations such as ways objects move **K.6D** observe and describe the ways that objects can move such as in a straight line, zigzag, up and down, back and forth, round and round, and fast and slow

Name _____

**straight**

**round and round**

Things move in different ways.

▶ Observe the pictures on the two pages. Describe the way objects can move–straight, round and round, up and down, back and forth, and zigzag. Color the arrows to show the direction in which things are moving.

Name _____

up and down

back and forth

zigzag

Things may change direction.

© Houghton Mifflin Harcourt Publishing Company  (l) ©John Lawrence Photography/Alamy; (tr) ©SnowyWelsh/Alamy; (br) ©Getty Images

Name _____

fast

Sometimes things move fast.

▶ Observe the pictures. Draw an X on the animal that can move fast.

Name _____

slow

Sometimes things move slowly.

© Houghton Mifflin Harcourt Publishing Company  (l) ©First Light/Alamy

▶ Observe the pictures. Draw something that can move slowly.
Describe how all the things move.

# Sum It Up!

● Circle the train that goes straight. ▲ Circle the marble that goes round and round. ■ Circle the animal that moves the most slowly.

# Using Magnets

Engineers design things that use magnets.
Sometimes using a magnet solves a problem.

**TEKS** **K.3A** identify and explain a problem ... and propose a solution in his/her own words **K.4A** collect information using tools, including ... magnets **K.6B** explore interactions between magnets and various materials

Physical Science • S.T.E.M. • Using Magnets  **61**

How can you use a magnet to solve a problem?

▶ Think of a problem you can solve by using a magnet. Draw the way the magnet solves the problem. Talk about your picture.

# Rocks

rocks

**TEKS** **K.2D** record and organize data and observations using pictures, numbers, and words **K.7A** observe, describe, compare, and sort rocks by size, shape, color, and texture

**different sizes**

**different shapes**

Rocks are nonliving things.

Rocks can be different sizes, shapes, colors, and textures.

▶ Observe the rocks in the first picture. Describe their sizes. Circle the smallest rock. Then observe the rocks in the second picture. Describe and compare their shapes. Draw an X on the square rock.

Name _____

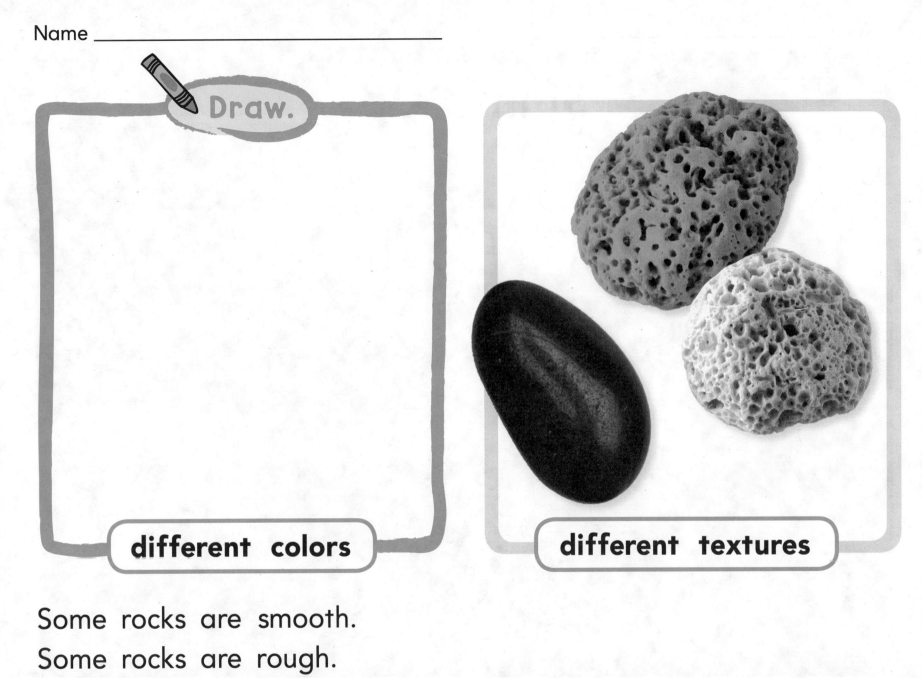

Draw.

**different colors**

**different textures**

Some rocks are smooth.
Some rocks are rough.

▶ Observe the color of the rocks on the two pages. Describe and compare the colors. Draw a brown rock, a gray rock, and a pink rock. Then observe the rocks in the second picture. Describe and compare their textures, or the way they feel. Circle the rough rocks. Draw an X on the smooth rock.

# Sum It Up!

Draw an X on each rock.

# Water

water

**TEKS** **K.2D** record and organize data and observations using pictures, numbers, and words **K.7B** observe and describe physical properties of natural sources of water, including color and clarity

Name _____

river

lake

ocean

Water is found in rivers, lakes, and oceans.
Water can look blue, green, or gray.

▶ Water is found in natural sources such as rivers, lakes, and oceans.
Draw an X on the river. Observe the pictures on the two pages.
Describe the color of the water in each picture.

Name _____

pond

**Draw.**

Clean water is clear.

Is the water in this pond clear?

▶ Describe (the clarity of) the water. Draw a pond with clear water.
Draw fish you can see when you look in the water.

# Sum It Up!

● Color the water blue. ▲ Color the water gray. ■ Color the water blue if it is clear. ★ Draw fish in the clear pond.

# Natural Resources

rock

water

soil

© Houghton Mifflin Harcourt Publishing Company  (bkgd) ©Lester Lefkowitz/CORBIS; (i) ©Jon Arnold Images Ltd/Alamy; (c) ©Getty Images

**TEKS** **K.1C** demonstrate how to use, conserve, and dispose of natural resources and materials such as conserving water and reusing or recycling paper, plastic, and metal **K.2D** record and organize data and observations using pictures, numbers, and words **K.7C** give examples of ways rock, soil, and water are useful

Unit 6 • Lesson 16
How Do We Use and Conserve Natural Resources?

71

Name _____

carrots

carrots growing in soil

Soil is a natural resource.
Most plants need soil to grow.
Many plants are food for people.

▶ Tell how soil is being used in the pictures. Give examples of other ways soil is useful. Draw an X on carrots growing in the soil.

Name _____

bridge

Draw.

Rocks are a natural resource.
We use rocks to make things.

► Tell how rocks are being used in the picture. Give examples of
other ways rocks are useful. Draw something made from rock.

Name _____

**We drink water.**

Water is a natural resource.
We need water to live.

Draw.

▶ Tell how water is being used in the picture. Give examples of other ways water is useful. Draw a way to use water.

**Turn off water after use.**

We should use water carefully.

We should use all natural resources carefully.

▶ Demonstrate how to use natural resources carefully (conserve).
Draw another way to use a natural resource carefully.

Name _____

reusing a can

reusing a tire

© Houghton Mifflin Harcourt Publishing Company  (l) Getty Images

We use materials and resources.
Then we dispose of them.
We can reuse materials and resources.

▶ Demonstrate ways we use materials such as paper, plastic, and metal. Circle a way a metal can is being reused.

Name _____

**recycling plastic**

**recycling cans**

We recycle plastic bottles and cans.

We use old bottles to make new things.

We use old cans to make new things.

▶ In each picture, circle something being recycled.

# Sum It Up!

● Circle the picture of soil being used.
  Circle the picture of water being used carefully.
■ Circle the picture of something being recycled.

# Weather

sunny

snowy

rainy

cloudy

windy

**TEKS** **K.2D** record and organize data and observations using pictures, numbers, and words **K.8A** observe and describe weather changes from day to day and over seasons

**cloudy weather**

Weather changes from day to day.
Some days are cloudy.
Some days are sunny.

**sunny weather**

▶ Circle the cloudy day. Observe today's weather and describe it. Discuss the weather over the past few days. Describe how the weather changed from day to day.

Name _____

**Draw.**

**windy weather**

Some days are windy.
Is it windy today?
Was it windy yesterday?

▶ Draw a tree on a windy day. Discuss whether it is windy today where
you live and if it was windy yesterday.

Name _____

rainy weather

Draw.

Some days are rainy.
On a rainy day, we play inside.

▶ Draw something you like to do on a rainy day. Discuss whether it has rained during the last week.

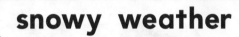

snowy weather

Some days are snowy.
Snowy days are cold.

▶ Circle the children playing in the snowy weather. Discuss whether it
ever snows where you live.

# Sum It Up!

●

▲

■

● Circle the snowy weather. ▲ Circle the rainy weather.
■ Circle the sunny weather.

# Measuring Weather

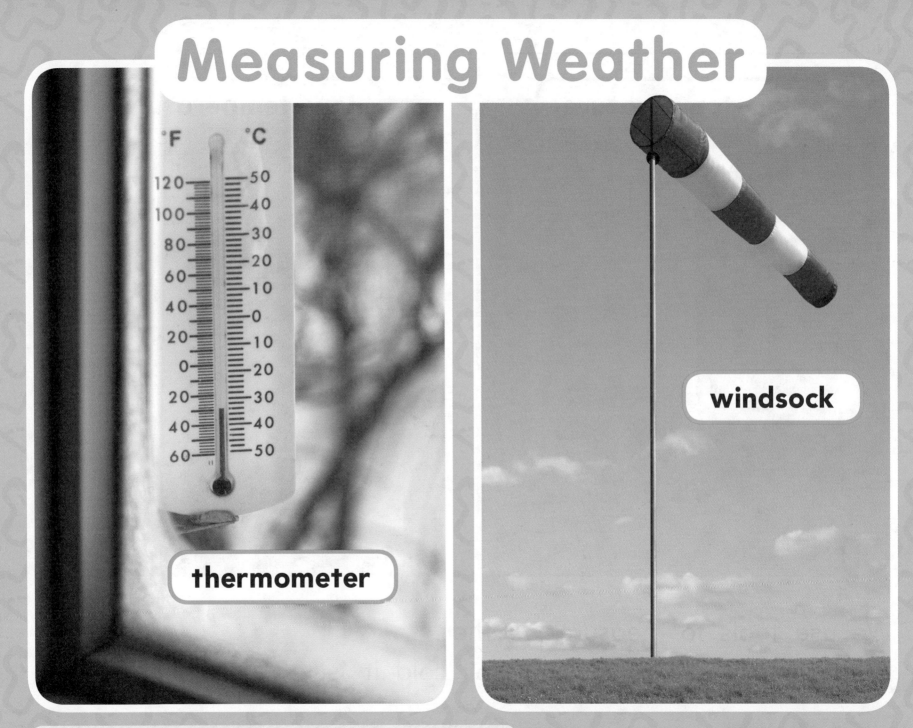

thermometer

windsock

**TEKS** **K.2D** record and organize data and observations using pictures, numbers, and words **K.4A** collect information using ... weather instruments such as demonstration thermometers and wind socks ...

high temperature

low temperature

We use tools to measure weather.
A thermometer tells how hot or cold it is.

▶ You can collect information about weather by using a thermometer. Discuss what a thermometer tells about weather. Circle the thermometer that shows a low temperature.

Name _____

**not windy**

**windy**

Draw.

A windsock shows if it is windy.

▶ You can collect information about weather by using a windsock. Discuss what a windsock tells about weather. Draw a windsock on a windy day. Draw a line from the word "windy" to your picture.

# Sum It Up!

● ▲ ■ Circle the tool each child could use to measure the weather shown.

# Seasons

**spring**

**summer**

**winter**

**fall**

**TEKS** **K.2D** record and organize data and observations using pictures, numbers, and words **K.3B** make predictions based on observable patterns in nature such as the shapes of leaves **K.8A** observe and describe weather changes from day to day and over seasons **K.8B** identify events that have repeating patterns, including seasons of the year and day and night

Name _____

spring

The seasons follow a pattern.
In spring, animals are born or hatched.
Warm weather helps plants grow.

▶ Observe the picture that shows spring. Circle the young animals.
Describe the kind of weather spring has.

© Houghton Mifflin Harcourt Publishing Company   (bkgd) ©David Aubrey/Photo Researchers, Inc.

Name _____

summer

Summer comes after spring.
In summer, plants grow bigger.
Young animals grow and learn.

▶ Observe the picture that shows summer. Circle the young deer doing
what its mother is doing. Describe the kind of weather summer has.

Name _____

fall

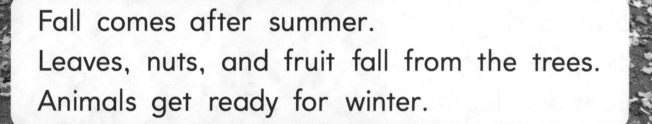

Fall comes after summer.
Leaves, nuts, and fruit fall from the trees.
Animals get ready for winter.

▶ Observe the picture that shows fall. Circle the animal getting ready for winter. Describe the kind of weather fall has.

Name _____

winter

Winter comes after fall.
Many trees lose all their leaves.
Some animals change in winter.

► Observe the picture that shows winter. Describe the kind of weather winter
has where you live. Discuss why the order of the seasons follows a pattern.
Predict the weather changes that will occur throughout a year.

# Sum It Up!

Draw what the tree looks like in spring, summer, fall, and winter.
Explain what the arrows show.

# Day Sky

sky

sun

clouds

**TEKS** **K.2D** record and organize data and observations using pictures, numbers, and words **K.8C** observe, describe, and illustrate objects in the sky such as the clouds, Moon, and stars, including the Sun

Name _____

| morning | noon | afternoon |

We see the sun in the sky during the day.

We also see clouds and other objects in the sky.

During the day, the sun seems to move across the sky.

© Houghton Mifflin Harcourt Publishing Company

▶ Observe the objects in the sky. Circle the sun in each picture. Describe where the sun is in each picture.

Name _____

far

Draw.

near

Objects near Earth look big.
Objects far from Earth look small.

▶ Observe the objects in the sky. Draw (illustrate) the sky during the day.

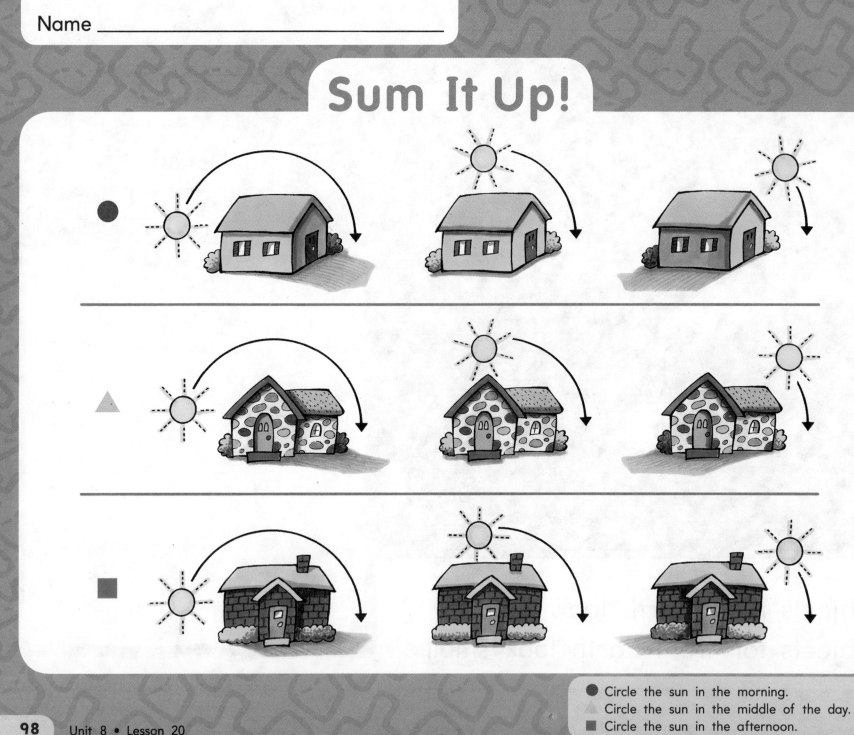

# Sum It Up!

● Circle the sun in the morning.
△ Circle the sun in the middle of the day.
■ Circle the sun in the afternoon.

# Night Sky

stars

moon

**TEKS** **K.2D** record and organize data and observations using pictures, numbers, and words **K.3B** make predictions based on observable patterns in nature ... **K.8B** identify events that have repeating patterns, including seasons of the year and day and night **K.8C** observe, describe, and illustrate objects in the sky such as the clouds, Moon, and stars, including the Sun

Name _____

**stars**

**moon**

Draw.

Night follows day.
At night we may see stars in the sky.
On many nights we see the moon.

▶ Observe and describe the objects in the night sky. Draw (illustrate) the moon.

Name _____

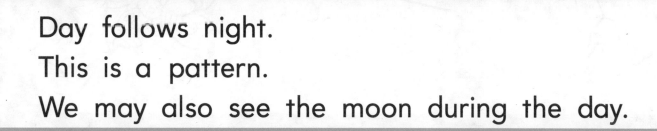

Day follows night.

This is a pattern.

We may also see the moon during the day.

▶ Circle the moon. Draw (illustrate) the sun in the day sky. Predict what
will follow day. Discuss why day and night have a repeating pattern.

Name _____

# Sum It Up!

● Draw (illustrate) the day sky.
▲ Draw (illustrate) the night sky.

# Recycling Paper

We can recycle paper.
We collect used paper.
New paper is made from it.

**paper being recycled**

**paper to be recycled**

**recycled paper**

© Houghton Mifflin Harcourt Publishing Company   (l) ©Photodisc/Getty Images; (bl) ©Lourens Smak/Alamy Images; (br) ©Ted Foxx/Alamy Images

**TEKS** **K.1C** demonstrate how to use, conserve, and dispose of natural resources and materials such as conserving water and reusing or recycling paper, plastic, and metal **K.3A** identify and explain a problem such as the impact of littering on the playground and propose a solution in his/her own words

▶ Tell why wasting paper is a problem. Demonstrate how you should dispose of used paper. Circle the things that can be made from recycled paper.

# Living and Nonliving

living things

nonliving things

TEKS K.2D record and organize data and observations using pictures, numbers, and words K.9A differentiate between living and nonliving things based upon whether they have basic needs and produce offspring K.9B examine evidence that living organisms have basic needs … K.10C identify ways that young plants resemble the parent plant

water

food

place to live

Living things need air, food, and water.
They also need a place to live.
Do nonliving things need these?

▶ Observe the pictures. Tell how you know they show living things. Discuss what living things need. Tell how you know. Circle the animal getting food.

Name _____

**new plant**

**ducks**

Draw.

Plants can make more plants.
Animals can have young.
Can nonliving things do this?

© Houghton Mifflin Harcourt Publishing Company   (l) ©Ashway/Alamy;  (r) ©Janusz Wrobel/Alamy

▶ A living thing looks like its parent. A plant looks like its
parent plant. Draw a young plant and its parent plant.

Name _____

# Sum It Up!

● Circle the living thing.   ▲ Circle the nonliving thing.

# Many Animals

**fur**

**feathers**

**scales**

**TEKS** **K.2D** record and organize data and observations using pictures, numbers, and words **K.10A** sort ... animals into groups based on physical characteristics such as color, size, body covering, or leaf shape **K.10B** identify ... parts of animals such as head, eyes, and limbs

Name _____

**blue jay**

**ladybug**

**elephant**

Animals have different shapes and sizes.
Some animals have bright colors.

▶ Circle the blue animal. Draw a line under the smallest animal.
Draw an X on the animal that has a trunk.

Name _____

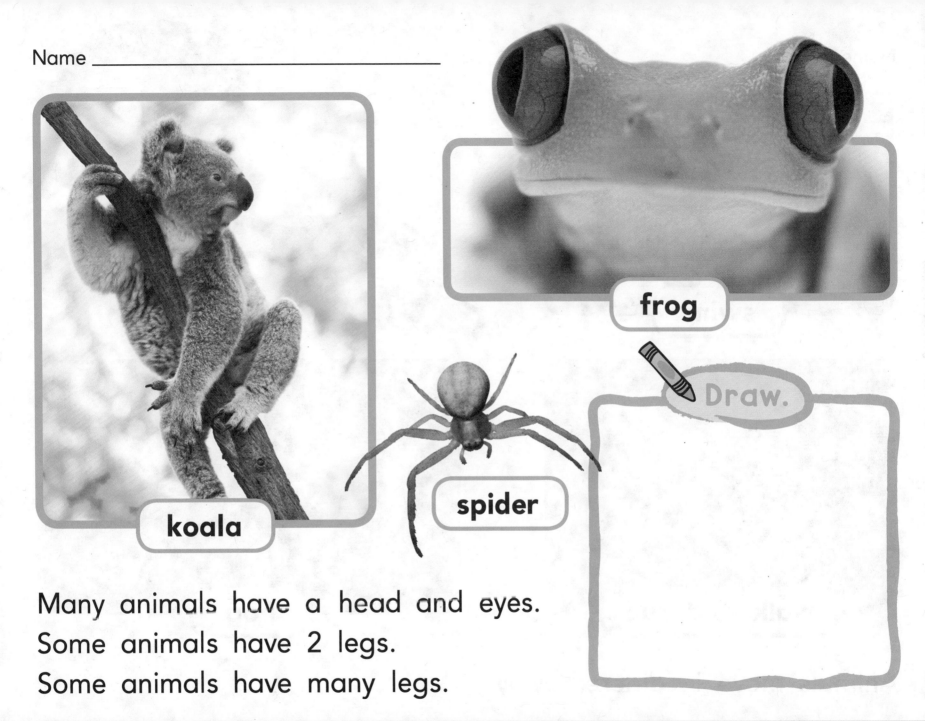

koala

frog

spider

Draw.

Many animals have a head and eyes.

Some animals have 2 legs.

Some animals have many legs.

▶ Circle the animal that has 8 legs. Draw the head and eyes of an animal.

Name _____

swim

crawl

walk and run

hop

Animals move in different ways.

▶ Circle the animal that crawls.

Draw.

fly

Which animal hops?

Which animal swims?

Which animal walks and runs?

© Houghton Mifflin Harcourt Publishing Company   ©Lisa Charles Watson/Getty Images

▶ Draw an animal that has wings.

# Sum It Up!

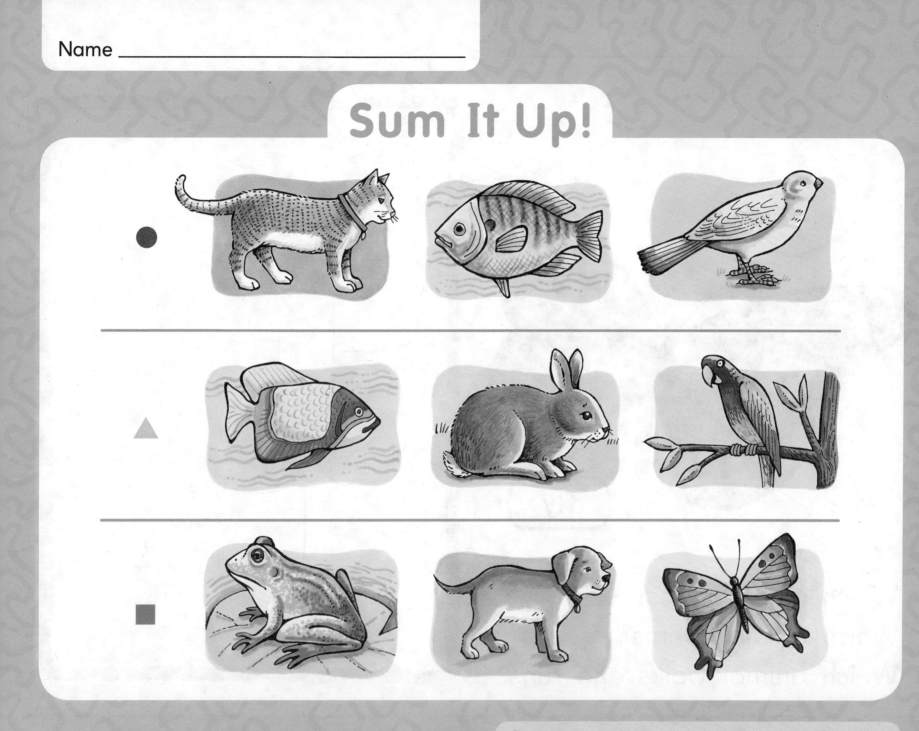

● Circle the animal that has four legs.  ▲ Circle the animal that does not have legs.  ■ Circle the animal that flies.

# What Animals Need

food

air

water

shelter

**TEKS** **K.2D** record and organize data and observations using pictures, numbers, and words **K.9B** examine that living organisms have basic needs such as food, water, and shelter for animals ...

Name _____

shelter

water

food

Animals need food, water, and air — just like you.
Animals need shelter — just like you.

▶ Discuss what the bear needs. Tell how you know. Circle the bear getting food.

Name _____

food

Pets need people to give them food, water, and shelter.

► Discuss what the fish needs. Tell how you know. Draw a pet getting what it needs.

# Sum It Up!

Circle the things the squirrel needs.

# Plants with Leaves

tree

leaf

shrub

© Houghton Mifflin Harcourt Publishing Company   (l) ©Christine Douglas/Photo Researchers/Getty Images;   (cl) ©Michael P. Gadomski/Photo Researchers/Getty Images; (t) ©Yvette Cardozo/Photolibrary/Getty Images;   (cr) ©Yvette Cardozo/Photolibrary/Getty Images

**TEKS** **K.2D** record and organize data and observations using pictures, numbers, and words **K.4B** use senses as a tool of observation to identify properties and patterns of organisms, objects, and events in the environment **K.10A** sort plants ... into groups based on physical characteristics such as ... leaf shape **K.10B** identify parts of plants ... such as leaves ...

Name _____

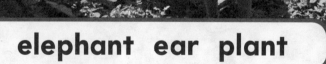

**elephant ear plant**

Many plants have leaves.
Some leaves are big.
Some leaves are small.

Draw.

▶ Look at the picture. Point to (identify) a leaf of the elephant
ear plant. Draw another leaf of an elephant ear plant.

Name _____

**oak**        **rose**        **pine**

Leaves have different shapes.

How can you describe these leaves' shapes?

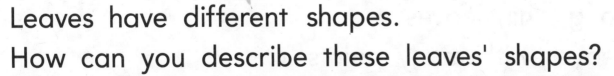

▶ Look at the pictures. Describe the shape of each plant's leaves.
Circle the name of the leaf that looks like a long, thin needle.

rounded

long, thin

many-pointed

Some plants have rounded leaves.
Some plants have long, thin leaves.
Some plants have leaves with many points.

© Houghton Mifflin Harcourt Publishing Company   (l) ©Chris Burrows/The Garden Picture Library/Dorling Kindersley/Getty Images; (c) ©Mathew Ward/Dorling Kindersley/Getty Images; (r) ©145/Ocean/Getty Images

▶ Look at the two pages. Sort the plants into groups based on leaf shape. Circle the plants that have rounded leaves. Underline the plants that have leaves with many points.

Name _____

Tell about the leaves of these plants.

# Sum It Up!

Sort the plants into groups based on leaf shape. ● Circle the plants with rounded leaves.    Underline the plants with long, thin leaves.

# What Plants Need

light

air

soil

space to grow

water

© Houghton Mifflin Harcourt Publishing Company ©Getty Images

**TEKS** **K.2D** record and organize data and observations using pictures, numbers, and words **K.9B** examine evidence that living organisms have basic needs such as ... air, water, nutrients, sunlight, and space for plants

Name _____

**water** | **no water** | Draw.

Plants need air, light, and water to live.

▶ Observe the plants. Discuss what they need. Tell how you know (examine evidence) that plants need water. Draw a plant getting water.

Name _____

Draw.

space to grow

soil

Plants need things from soil.
Plants need space to grow.

▶ Discuss why plants need nutrients from soil. Most plants get the light they need from the sun. Draw the sun.

# Sum It Up!

Draw a line to each thing the plant needs.

# Plants Grow and Change

seed

flower

sprout

seedling

adult plant

© Houghton Mifflin Harcourt Publishing Company   (l) ©iStop/Alamy;   (t) ©Papilio/Alamy;   (r) ©Nigel Cattlin/Alamy;   (b) ©Mark Boulton/Alamy

**TEKS** **K.2D** record and organize data and observations using pictures, numbers, and words **K.10C** identify ways that young plants resemble the parent plant **K.10D** observe changes that are part of a simple life cycle of a plant: seed, seedling, plant, flower, and fruit

Name _____

**seed**

**sprout**

**seedling**

A plant has a life cycle.
A plant changes as it grows.
A young plant is like its parent plant.

▶ Discuss what a life cycle is. Observe the changes in the life cycle of this plant. Circle the seed.

Name _____

Draw.

young tree

adult tree

▶ Draw the young tree that will grow into the adult tree in the picture.
Tell (identify) the ways this tree probably looks like its parent tree.

# Sum It Up!

Circle the seedling. Draw a line under the adult tree.

# Aquarium Design

People learn about animals at aquariums.
Engineers design places for the animals.
The animals get food, water, and shelter.

**aquarium exhibits**

**TEKS** **K.1C** demonstrate how to use ... natural resources **K.4A** collect information using ... materials to support observations of habitats of organisms such as terrariums and aquariums **K.9B** examine evidence that living organisms have basic needs such as food, water, and shelter for animals and air, water, nutrients, sunlight, and space for plants

Name _____

Design a home aquarium.

What animals will you have?

What plants will you use?

What else will you use?

▶ Discuss what animals and plants need. Draw a picture to show how you would design a home aquarium. Describe what it would look like.